WordPress Revealed
How to Build a Website, Get Visitors and Make Money (Even For Beginners)

D0823555

Matt Wolfe

Praise For WordPress Revealed and Matt Wolfe

"Whilst many people can claim to know Wordpress, not many have mastered it like Matt Wolfe. He is one of the very few people who can walk a complete beginner through ALL the steps they need to take to succeed and more importantly, profit from Wordpress. Matt Wolfe can teach you this because he has done it, time and time again. That's why he is the Wordpress "guru" and go to guy for many top business people and entrepreneurs. When he tells you something about Wordpress, listen."

Josh Bartlett

www.easyvideoplayer.com

"This is H O T !! I took about 90 days and studied what you taught…I did what you recommended and I set everything up the way you said. Saturday 8-4-12 at 4:03 PM EDT, I launched Aerial-Photography-Academy.com In our first 24 hours, we had $675 in sales. This is all before any promotion, YouTube video advertising…nothing, nada, zip, zero. This is truly remarkable. What you teach, the advice you give and the philosophy you prescribe is as solid and dependable as the North Star. At 63, a non technical schmo, went from zero to

Hero in 3 months. I just got up this morning to find my PayPal account heavy with cash…all while I slept. You said it would work if we did our part. Send me the Kool Aid….I'm drinking it!!! August 4 is my Independence Day from the man. I know my retirement and my future are secure. This would have been impossible without you. If you ever wonder if you have the power to change lives, rest assured…you do! Thank you Matt Wolfe."

David Rodwell

www.aerial-photography-academy.com

"This is by far the absolute best and in-depth book on Wordpress to date. Matt Wolfe takes you by the hand and shows you the EXACT steps to take from starting with absolutely no knowledge to a place where you're set up to make a living off of your new Wordpress website online. After being a long-term member of Matt's WordPressClassroom.com and him consulting on my business, he's been able to ramp up my once mediocre performing Wordpress site and raise it to a point where it brings in a consistent income of 5-figures per month for my business. Take Matt's advice in this book, it works."

Joe Fier

VideoSalesLab.com

Table of Contents

Introduction

Many people have wanted me to put out a book on WordPress from my point of view, using my experiences from it, and discussing the ways that I've used it to create a sustainable online business. I'm not quite sure why I resisted for so long, to be honest. If you combine all of the blog posts that I've written between 2005 and 2012, I probably have about ten books worth of content. Something about writing a book has just really intimidated me.

I've decided to take a stab at it and get my feet wet with a mini-book of sorts. This isn't an "end-all, be-all" guide to everything WordPress. Instead, I'm picking out the pieces that are most important and that will help as many people as possible get pointed in the right direction as soon as possible and I'm diving straight in to those topics.

In this "crash course" for WordPress, I'm going to spend my time answering the questions that people ask the most with as much depth and clarity as possible. I'm not talking about copying and pasting the frequently asked questions from the WordPress.org website either. I'm going to dive in to the stuff the people really want to know. Things like <u>what the best</u> <u>plugins are and why</u>, <u>how to drive traffic to a WordPress site</u>, and <u>what my favorite ways to make money with my sites are</u>.

I'm also going to spend some time discussing all of the various ways that WordPress can be used to build a sustainable and profitable long-term business. It's one thing to slap up ads on your site and make a little money out of it; however, building a business from a WordPress site is something entirely different. That's the difference between extra spending money and a lifetime of job security.

I'll admit that I'm not the best author in the world and you may find some grammar and spelling mistakes throughout the chapters in this book. Please bear with me as putting this guide together is already really far outside of my comfort zone. It's putting me "out there" and in the public more than most other projects I've done in the past. I am really excited, however, to share this information with a new audience and show a whole new generation of web entrepreneurs how powerful WordPress really can be. It's changed my life and allowed me to quit my job and I can't wait to give some insight in to what I've learned along the way.

About Me

I don't want this book to turn in to a biography so I will just briefly brush over who I am and what I've done over the past several years...

I will admit that I've been good with computers my whole life. I learned how to program in a language called Qbasic and a language called Assembly Language when I was about eleven years old. As soon I learned about the internet I started learning HTML so I could develop websites for myself. I would go to my favorite websites, download the website to my hard drive and then open it in notepad to reverse engineer how it was built.

I don't remember how old I was but I used to create a

whole bunch of free websites on all of those free hosting sites that popped up all over the place. Sites like Angelfire, Geocities, Tripod, and Homestead all appeared in the mid-nineties and allowed you to host free websites in exchange for them hosting ads on your sites. I created tons of websites on all of my favorite games and movies at the time and shared them in all my favorite message boards around the internet. This was my first entry in to website creation and traffic generation.

In about 2003, I was working for the family business, a shutter company in San Diego, California. The family knew I was good at creating websites and asked me to develop theirs. I took my time and made a really great, professional looking website for the business. The site was so good, in fact, that other companies actually contacted my parents to ask who did their site. My parents started referring me my first website clients.

I worked for the family business during the day while spending my evenings working on websites for clients and myself. In 2005 one of my website clients actually asked me if I had ever heard of WordPress. I told him that I didn't but that I'd definitely look in to it. This was the beginning of my pursuit to completely understand everything there is to know about WordPress.

I began shifting all of my client's sites and the family business's website to WordPress because it made creating websites <u>so</u> <u>dang</u> <u>simple</u>. Things that used to take me hours and hours to do now took minutes with WordPress.

In 2008 the economy was in a downward spiral and the housing market was crashing. Being in a business that sold window coverings for homes was not a great place to be. The company began to really struggle as people stopped purchasing new homes or opted for less expensive window covering options. In the struggle to stay afloat, the family made the decision to sell the business.

A new owner took over the company with a "crack the whip" mentality. He believed that threatening employees with violence and making sure that everyone feared for their jobs was the proper way to run a business. He had me calling up clients and doing really unethical things to try to land new business. At one point I was told that if I didn't lie for him about something that he would "make me and my family disappear". It was a very scary and stressful time.

In the evenings I would work on client sites to make

some extra money. Around this time I also became really interested in finance and investing. I set up my first niche blog in the personal finance space and starting selling advertising and banner space on the site. This started making me some real good extra spending money so I set up second and third niche blogs in the health space and the gardening space.

One day my boss's threats were just more than I could handle and I walked out the door never to return. I told myself that as long as I knew how to create websites for myself and if my clients kept referring work to me I'd be alright. I quit that job on May 21st, 2009. I can never forget that date because it was actually two days before my wedding day.

I pushed forward with my client business, working on referrals setting up websites for local businesses. My niche sites were making somewhere around $200-$300 per month and my client business brought in another $500 or $600. It was great to be working for myself but it definitely wasn't enough to pay the bills. I would need to figure out a way to ramp this all up or I'd have to go out and start looking for a new job.

In August of 2009, I started up The WordPress Classroom. This site was a result of so many people asking me how I was making the money I was making with these niche websites. I was getting multitudes of people asking the same questions over and over again... So much so that I decided to start a blog about WordPress to make tutorial videos and show people exactly how I was doing it.

I began promoting this new site inside forums and on other blogs. I began building a mailing list, grabbing emails in exchange for free training videos. Over just a couple months I built this mailing list to about 300 subscribers. When I finally opened the doors to the "Pro" membership, a paid version of my training tutorials, I sold 50 copies on the first day. I sold it at $27 and had my first "$1,000 Plus" day.

As I write this, it has been almost three years since I launched the WordPress Classroom. I still run it today. To date, I've had over 5,000 members go through the training and have lined up thousands of testimonials from people who have successfully managed to learn WordPress and set up sites for either themselves or for clients.

Over the last seven years, I've learned so much about WordPress and how to build a successful online business. I've set up at least twenty websites on the WordPress platform and have a team of outsourcers setting up even more for me constantly. Once I learned about how easy it is to create these sites and how easy it can actually be to monetize these sites, life has never been the same. I no longer have any insecurity about how my bills will be paid or if I'll ever have to look for a job again. Creating websites with WordPress has been a "game-changer" for me I'm and hoping, that with this guide, combined with some free bonus video training at The WordPress Classroom, it can be a game changer for you too.

How This Book Is Structured

Running a well-known training site at the WordPress Classroom, I get hundreds of questions every day, ranging from real basic setup questions to advanced traffic and monetization strategies. I've sifted through all the questions, compiled them, and organized them into a chart so that I could see which questions came up the most frequently.

I've broken down all the questions and split them in to categories so that you can skip around to exactly what you're looking for.

I've then given the most specific and detailed answers to each question that I could, and oftentimes included pictures where necessary. Some of the pictures may not show up so well on black and white eReaders. However, you should still be able to follow along closely to the instructions. I've also made free video tutorials available over at The WordPress Classroom that you can follow along with to better understand much of the training.

To watch many of the steps performed throughout this eBook in video form, check out the free seven day bonus training course at http://www.thewpclassroom.com/wprevealed/.

Towards the end of the book, I have also included several interviews from various experts that use WordPress to make their living. If there's one part of this book that everyone must read (beginner to advanced), this is the section. This is the part where you will learn real life examples from people "in the trenches", making WordPress work for them. You will learn what WordPress is truly capable of and the various ways that people have figured out how to generate an income from it. Do not skip this section.

Enjoy!

The Basics

What exactly is WordPress?

WordPress is a content management system. It's basically a platform that, once installed on your server, makes it insanely simple to create websites. In the old days, if you wanted to have a menu on your website with links to other pages on your website, you'd need to code that menu in to the page and duplicate that page over and over again to make sure all pages on your site looked the same. If you wanted to add or remove an item from a menu, you would have to edit every single one of those pages to make sure the item was removed from all the menus. Needless to say, it was real pain. With WordPress, you can edit that menu ONCE and it adjusts everything on all of your pages, giving your site a nice uniform look.

WordPress also has a huge open source community, meaning that people out there are actively working on new themes and plugins to improve the functionality of WordPress.

WordPress used to be primarily focused on creating

amazing blogs, however, it has evolved over time in to so much more than just a blogging platform. People use it for everything these days... From blogging, to ecommerce sites, to classifieds, to (my favorite) membership sites...

What are the differences between WordPress.com and WordPress.org?

There are really two ways that you can use WordPress. You can use WordPress.org, which is the self-hosted version of the platform, or you can use WordPress.com where they will actually host the site for you.

With WordPress.org, you will actually need your own hosting account and you install the WordPress platform on that hosting account. You have full control over what is posted on your site and you have a ton of options for plugins and themes to really customize what the site is capable of. WordPress.org self-hosted sites are what you would want to use if you plan to do things like membership sites, ecommerce sites, classified sites, and even monetized niche blogs because full control of the site and its contents are solely in your hands. The majority of this book focuses on building sites around your own hosting company and using WordPress.org.

WordPress.com, on the other hand, is hosted on WordPress's servers. You don't have to pay for hosting and it's completely free to setup. The downside is that there are restrictions to what you can and can't do with your site. You have a very limited amount of plugins and themes to choose from when designing your site, and it's much more difficult to diversify the ways in which you monetize the site.

I recommend that anyone who really wants to make a business out of using WordPress, set up their site on their own hosting, with their own domain, using the platform downloaded from WordPress.org. You'll save yourself so many headaches with customization and you'll look that much more professional because you can remove the WordPress branding if you choose to do so. I explain how to go about setting up hosting and domains in the section called "How do I actually install WordPress?".

What are the benefits of using WordPress?

There are a ton of benefits to using WordPress, some of which I already mentioned. In general, WordPress simply makes creating websites so much easier than it used to be. Pretty much anyone can have a website online within minutes without knowing anything about design or HTML code. It's point and click simple to get your websites online. It's so simple, I've heard of a 5 year old kid setting up a site with WordPress.

WordPress is search engine friendly. Because WordPress creates a ton of pages for you and updates all the existing pages when a new page is created, the search engines absolutely love it. So many people have created blogs with WordPress and began seeing their site in the search results within days without any extra search engine optimization on the page at all.

WordPress has thousands and thousands of themes you can use to change the look and feel of the site. The best part is that, if you change out a theme, the content of your site and all of your menus stay intact. You don't have to worry about losing any data on your site when you change the look. It is so simple, in fact, that you can test new themes whenever you feel like it without fear that it's going to mess up the existing content on your site. I test new themes constantly.

WordPress has thousands of plugins that extend the functionality of the site. Simply adding various plugins can change your site from a blog to a membership site or from a simple business site to a fully integrated ecommerce site, ready to take orders right from the homepage.

The benefits of WordPress are far too numerous to count. However, I think the real benefits will become more and more apparent throughout the course of this book. So keep reading to learn everything that WordPress is capable of.

What are some big name sites that use WordPress?

You would probably be shocked to learn of some of the really big sites that are powered by WordPress. The fact that it is so simple to use and has so much functionality makes it an ideal choice for almost every website.

Many popular blogs and news sites are powered by WordPress like The Wall Street Journal, Time Magazine, TED, CNN, UPS, Tech Crunch and more. You'll also find that almost all celebrity sites are using WordPress as well. Check out http://vip.wordpress.com/clients/ to get a little list of some really popular websites that are powered by WordPress.

How do I actually install WordPress?

WordPress is quite simple to install and literally takes minutes to do. However, there are a couple things you need before we can get to the process.

To begin, you're going to need a hosting account. This is the server space on the internet where all the website data is stored. If you're going to create a self-hosted WordPress blog, server space is mandatory. Personally, I use a hosting company called HostGator. It costs somewhere around $10/month and is among the least expensive you'll find. To top that off, if you use the coupon code "LearnToBlog", you'll receive an extra 25% off. So you can't go wrong with that hosting.

While purchasing your hosting account, you'll want to select a <u>domain name</u> as well. This is where your site will be located. For example, my site is located at www.TheWPClassroom.com. TheWPClassroom.com is my domain name. So select a domain name for your site during checkout with HostGator.

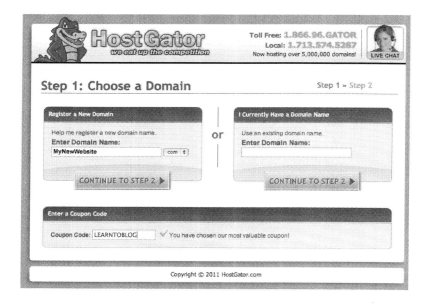

Once you've purchased your hosting account, you'll receive login details in your email inbox to login to something called Cpanel. This is your <u>control panel</u> where you will install Wordpress.

Once logged in to Cpanel, scroll down and look for the blue smiley face with the word "Fantastico" underneath it. Click this icon.

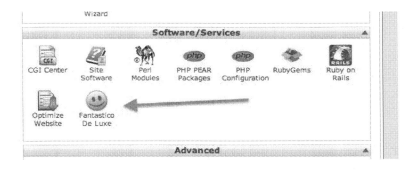

Once you click on the Fantastico icon, select WordPress on the page that follows. Click "New Installation".

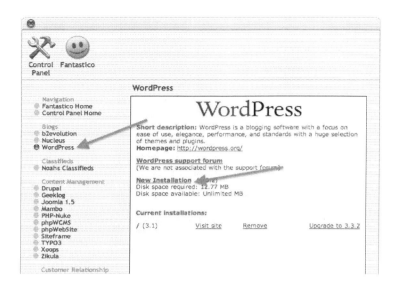

On the screen that follows, you will see some options. You should an area that says "Install on domain" with a box next to it that shows your domain name that you just purchased. Below that you'll see "Install in directory". If you want your blog to be located at www.yourdomain.com then leave "Install in directory" blank. However, if you want it located on a sub-domain like www.yourdomain.com/blog, you would type the word "blog" in the box next to "Install on directory". Choose a username and password that you want to use to login to WordPress and fill in your site details. Once you've done those steps, you can click "Install WordPress" to move on.

After clicking "Install WordPress", you'll see another screen confirming some installation details. Click "Finish Installation" and you'll be ready to go.

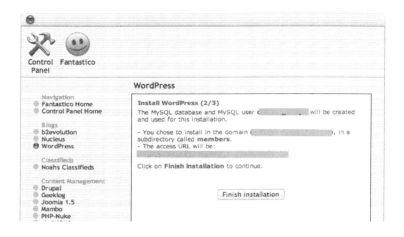

You can also follow along to the tutorial video on day 2 of the free training available at The WordPress Classroom. http://www.thewpclassroom.com/wprevealed/

How do I login to the dashboard of my new website?

Once you've got WordPress installed, you can always access your dashboard by going to http://yourdomain.com/wp-admin/. Once you are there you can enter the username and password that we just created in the previous installation steps.

From this point on, when I mention "login to your WordPress dashboard", I am referring to this step. Simply navigate to the link above on your own domain and login to your WordPress dashboard.

Once I'm in my WordPress dashboard, what do I do?

Now that you've successfully installed WordPress, you can start doing the fun part. You get to start editing and tweaking the look and functionality of your site. This is where we start playing with themes and plugins to get the exact site that you've always wanted.

We're going to get to the details of setting up your theme and your plugins in just a minute. However, let's continue covering some of the basics of WordPress before we push too much further.

How do I write a blog post?

Creating a blog post is really simple and it will probably be the task that you find yourself doing the most with your blog. Making sure that you're constantly creating new content that's relevant and interesting is what's going to keep people coming back over and over again. So posting often is essential.

Once you're in your WordPress dashboard, simply click

on "Posts" and then "Add New" from the menu on the left. You can then choose a title, write your blog post and publish it for the world to see.

What's the difference between a page and a post?

Something that people often confuse is the difference between a post and page. They both serve different purposes but look very similar.

The best explanation I can give is that pages are where you would put static content that never really changes. People often link to their pages in the header menu or in their sidebar menu because it is content that they expect people to view frequently. The most common example is the "About me" page. You would create a page with details about yourself, link to it in a menu, and it rarely changes.

A blog post on the other hand is content that is typically listed in reverse-chronological order on your website. Every time you create a new blog post it appears above the previous post on your blog's page. As you write more and more blog posts, your older posts move down the page and eventually drop off the front page completely.

Blog posts are typically more social as well. When someone views a blog post, in most cases, readers can leave comments below the post and interact with the writer and the blog's other readers. There is typically no commenting on pages.

For a good example of posts vs. pages, have a look at BusinessAndBlogs.com. If you click on one of the links on the front page for an article I've recently written, you are clicking in to a blog post. If you click on the "About Me' link at the top of the page, you are clicking in to a blog page. Visualizing it on a blog may help solidify the concept.

What are tags and categories?

Tags and categories are often confused with each other as well. This is for good reason too because, over time, the distinction has become more and more blurred. I have some blogs where I don't even bother using tags at all because just using categories on my posts is enough.

When creating a new blog post in WordPress, you'll see the options to add categories and add tags to an individual post over in the menu on the right. These are basically to help keep relevant content grouped together when readers of your blog are browsing for information. Both tags and categories serve this exact purpose.

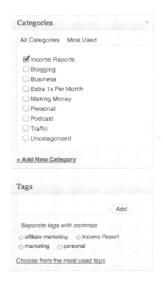

The way I use tags and categories is by choosing only one category for a blog post and then using multiple tags for each blog post. The category is the broader topic that I'm discussing, the tags are the relevant keywords mentioned in that post that could also be associated with that post.

For example, let's say I'm writing a blog post about how to generate traffic to a website using Facebook. For this blog post my category would probably be "Traffic Techniques". The tags I would use on this post would be "Traffic, Facebook, Social Media, Marketing" and any other relevant topics I may have mentioned throughout that post.

Now if someone visits my site, they could look at all the posts in a specific category or all the posts under a specific tag. The "Traffic Techniques" category may have posts about Facebook, search engine optimization, forum marketing, and all sorts of other traffic techniques. The "Facebook" tag, on the other hand, would only have blog posts specific to Facebook.

Categories and tags are simply a way to organize the content on your blog in to a way that makes it easier for readers to find more details on specific topics that you discuss.

What is a widget?

Often times people confuse widgets and plugins. They actually are not the same thing. I'll get in to detail about plugins in just a few minutes but it's definitely important to understand what a widget is first.

Widgets control the look of your sidebar. The menus on the left or right side of your website that contain links, or ads, or listings of your recent posts, etc... These are all controlled through widgets.

While in your WordPress dashboard, if you click on
"Appearance" and then "Widgets" from the menu on the left,
you'll see where you control your widgets.

On the right side of the screen you can see a listing of
your sidebars. In the middle of your screen you can see the
widgets that are available to put in to your sidebars.

You can simply drag and drop widgets over to the
sidebar to see them appear on your blog. For example, if I want
to show a listing of all my blog's categories in my sidebar, I'd
click on the "Categories" box in the middle of the screen and
drag that box over in to my sidebar. I'd then take a look at my
site to see my categories neatly listed on my blog's sidebar.

Themes

What is a theme?

WordPress themes are one of the things that make WordPress so powerful. Themes dictate the look, layout, and some of the functionality of your website.

In the old days, when you wanted to change the look of a website, you basically had to start from scratch. Each page on your website needed to be remade, all the content had to be copied from the old site and pasted in to the new site, and there were usually a lot of growing pains with bugs and issues popping up with the new site design.

With WordPress, however, you can swap out themes at will and completely change the look and feel of your site without dealing with all the headaches of recreating an entire site. Just choose a new theme, upload it, activate it, and your entire site has a completely new look. It's that simple.

How do you find new themes?

There are many places to find new themes for your website. It really depends on what you are trying to accomplish that dictates the best place to start looking for the perfect theme. Some themes are free and some you're going to need to pay for. It all depends on what you are going for.

For free themes, you can simply do a search from within your WordPress dashboard.

If you click on "Appearance" and then "Themes" in the left menu inside your dashboard, you will see a tab at the top that says "Install Theme." Clicking this tab brings up a little search engine to search for free themes for your website.

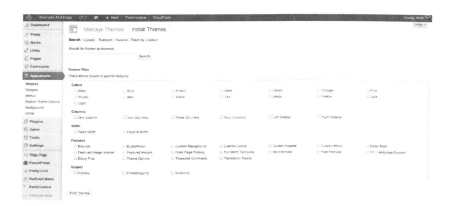

Personally, I've never had much luck finding themes that I was real happy with through this little internal WordPress search engine. None of them seem to have the professionalism that I like to go for with my websites. However, if you search hard enough, you may find some gems buried within.

Another option to find free themes is to simply do a search on Google for "Free WordPress Themes". You will find all sorts of sites that list free themes that you can easily install on your website. If I'm hunting for a free theme, I typically have much better luck finding quality themes via Google than I do from the internal WordPress theme search.

If you really want to get some quality themes, I recommend diving into more premium themes. These are usually much more professional looking, have much more functionality built in and have more built in customization options. However, premium themes are almost never free.

Some of my favorite resources for premium themes are ThemeForest.net, WooThemes.com, and Theme-Junkie.com. In fact, as of writing this, the current theme on Business and Blogs is a theme from Theme-Junkie.

Themes like Thesis and FlexTheme are also really great because they offer a great amount of customization. Personally, I don't like spending all the time customizing the themes myself in the settings so I like to look for a theme that already looks the way I want it from a place like Theme Forest or Theme-Junkie.

What theme do you recommend?

Again, this is a tough question to answer because themes vary depending on the goal. The theme that's currently installed on Business and Blogs is called Big Foot and I purchased it from Theme-Junkie. It works great for my purposes but I wouldn't recommend it for everyone.

If you're trying to use your WordPress website to create sales pages or squeeze pages (a page designed to collect email addresses) a theme called Optimize Press is the best I've found. It makes awesome and professional pages for the purpose of selling a product or specifically building a list.

If your goal is to set up a web presence for your business, I'd take a look at Theme Forest under the corporate themes. There are some amazing themes that will give your business site the professional feel that you are looking for.

Maybe you're trying to create an ecommerce site to sell dolls or antique furniture. Theme Forest has loads of ecommerce specific themes.

It may require a little bit of hunting and research to get the perfect theme for your website. Theme Forest, Theme-Junkie, and Woo Themes all offer an insanely large amount of themes to browse through for pretty much any situation I could imagine. That's where I'd start.

Keep an eye out on sites that you really like the look of as well. Many times you can find the name of the theme in the footer. If not, you can always attempt to contact the site owner and ask them what theme they're using. If they're cool, they'll spill the beans.

How do I install a custom theme?

Finding a theme from an external site (other than using the built-in theme search) requires a couple of extra steps to get it installed. It's still really simple but it will take a couple more steps.

Once you find the theme you like and purchase it, you will be able to download it to your hard drive as a .zip file. Once you've downloaded it, don't bother unzipping it. Just save the zip file on your computer in a location you can remember.

Log in to your WordPress dashboard and click on "Appearance" and then "Themes" from the menu on the left.

On the next screen, click on the "Install Themes" tab at the top of the screen.

Directly above the search box, you'll see a little menu with "Search | Upload | Featured...". Click on the "Upload" link.

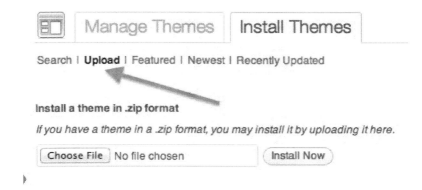

On this screen you can now click "Choose File", find your file, and click "Install Now". Once the theme is installed, click the button to activate the theme and then browse to your site's web address to see your awesome new theme up and running on your site.

How do I add a custom header?

This is another really complicated question. Pretty much every theme available has a slightly different way of adding a custom header.

Most premium themes actually add a new menu item to your dashboard to customize the theme. There's usually an option to upload a custom header within this customization area. However, many custom themes and most free themes don't offer this functionality.

If you're using the default theme that is installed when you first set up WordPress, you can actually click on "Appearance" and then "Header" from the menu on the left to select a custom header image.

If there's no option from within your theme to customize the header, things get a bit more complicated and the method to change out the header can vary from theme to theme and, in most cases, will require you (or someone else) to edit some lines of code.

In this scenario, if you're not comfortable messing with code a little bit, I highly recommend going to a place like odesk.com or elance.com and hiring someone to fix this for you. You can probably expect to pay somewhere around $10 - $20 for this quick fix.

However, if you want to get your hands dirty, you can attempt to tweak the header yourself...

Feel free to skip this part if you've decided to take the safe and smart route and just plan to outsource the swapping of your header...

Swapping out the header

I'll warn you again that every theme is different and these directions may not work for your theme. This is just a basic overview and a "most-case-scenario" for swapping out the header on a custom theme...

So the first thing we need to do is figure out how the header was added to your site. Was it done inside the CSS style sheet or inside the header.php file. (If the tech speak scares you, don't worry... I'll show you what to do).

From your blog's homepage, view the source of the page. In some browsers you can right-click and select "view source" and in some browsers it will be in one of the menus at the top of the browser. Figure out how to view source and look at the source of your blog's home page.

While viewing the source, do a search for the word "header". You can usually hit command + f or control-f to start a search.

Close to that header text that you just found, you may see something that looks like this "<img src="http://www.yourwebsite.com/wp-content/themes/themename/custom/images/header.jpg">". It obviously won't say exactly that but it may say something similar.

If you see the above text or something similar, it usually means that your header image can be edited from within the header.php file. If you don't see anything like that at all, it often times means your header can be edited from the stylesheet.css file.

If your theme doesn't come with a header at all, this won't work. You will probably want to hire someone instead. I recommend that if you want to use a custom header, you find a theme that has a header in it already that you can change out. It makes it much easier.

Now, from within your WordPress dashboard, select "Media" and "Add New" from the menu on the left side. Click the button at the top that says "Add New". Find the header image that you want to use and drop it on to the screen.

After the file has uploaded, you will see a section that says "File URL" with a long URL in the box next to it. Copy this URL and paste it in to a notepad. You will need it in just a minute.

If we determined that your header can be edited from within the header.php file, click on "Appearance" and then "Editor" from the menu on the left inside your dashboard. On the right side click on the link that says "Header".

Within this file, look for a code similar to the one that was mentioned above: http://www.yourwebsite.com/wp-content/themes/themename/custom/images/header.jpg, and replace the URL that is there with the URL of the one you just pasted in to a notepad. This should replace the old header with your new one.

If we determined earlier that your header can be edited from within the stylesheet.css, click on "Appearance" and then "Editor" from the menu on the left inside your dashboard. On the right side click on the link that says "Stylesheet".

From within this screen, do a search for the word "header". Somewhere near where you find the header code, you will see a URL similar to the one I mentioned earlier. Replace that URL with the one that you copied to a notepad. This should replace your header with the new one.

I can't stress enough that you should probably hire someone to do this if you are uncomfortable with code. These instructions won't work with all sites but provides a basic overview for how to do it with most sites.

I was real hesitant to even include these instructions in this book. However, this is probably the number one most asked question that I receive. I can't leave out instructions for probably THE most asked question... So, therefore, you get my best possible explanation of how to do it on most WordPress sites.

Plugins

What is a plugin?

Plugins are something that make WordPress super powerful. They are essentially little add-ons for your site that increase the functionality. You can basically install these plugins with a few clicks of the mouse and have all new features and functions for your website.

There are plugins to turn your website in to a membership site, plugins for affiliate marketing, plugins for search engine optimization, plugins to add extra security and so much more.

The beauty of WordPress plugins is that they add new functionality and new coding to your website without you having to touch the code yourself. You simply install the plugin, activate it, and you are ready to go.

A word of caution, however... Most WordPress plugins are free plugins made by individuals that want to support and grow the capabilities of WordPress. Being free, these plugins rarely have support. If you can't get a plugin to work, chances are, there's not going to be any customer support to contact to get things working again. Most plugins, however, do have instructions and by following these instructions you will usually have no issues adding the functionality you were hoping to add.

How do you find new plugins?

Similar to WordPress themes, there are free plugins available and there are premium plugins available. The vast majority of the things people want to do with their websites can be handled with free plugins. People looking to get more advanced functionality like creating membership sites or building out classified sites may need to look towards premium plugins to accomplish this.

Just like with free WordPress themes, you can actually do a search for free WordPress plugins from directly within your WordPress dashboard.

Simply login to your dashboard, select "Plugins" from the menu on the left and then select "Add New". You will be taken to the internal WordPress plugin search engine to find any free plugins that you'd like.

You can basically type the function that you're looking to accomplish with your website and click "Search Plugins" to find what you're looking for.

For example, if I'm interested in finding a plugin that adds a contact form on to my blog, I'd type "contact form" in to the search box and click "Search Plugins". Doing this will result in a list of several plugins that will allow me to add a contact form on to my blog. Simply read the details of each plugin until you find one that seems to suit the exact needs you are looking for.

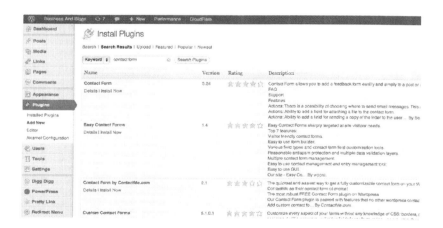

When it comes to more advanced (premium) plugins, there really isn't a specific search engine to find these. In most cases, I would just do a Google search for the function I'm looking for and the phrase "WordPress plugin".

For example, if I'm looking for a plugin that turns my website in to a membership site, I'd do a Google search for the term "Membership Site WordPress Plugin". That search results in many premium plugins that will help me turn my website into a membership site.

How do I install a plugin?

To install a free plugin from within the WordPress dashboard's plugin search, simply find the plugin you want to install and click the "Install Now" link directly below the name of the WordPress plugin.

A box will pop up confirming that you want to install this plugin. Click the button to confirm that you do, in fact, want to install the plugin. You will see some text appear on the screen followed by "Successfully installed the plugin..."

Click "Activate Plugin" and your new plugin will be live and ready.

Once the plugin is installed, it will probably have some sort of settings that need to be adjusted. In most cases, you can click on "Settings" in the menu on the left side of your dashboard and find the plugin's name to adjust the settings. If you don't see the plugin's name under "Settings", look under "Tools" or "Appearance". Some plugins put their settings link in different spots on the menu.

If you purchase a plugin from an external website and want to install it on your blog there are a couple extra steps involved.

Typically, if you purchase a plugin from an external site, you will receive a .zip file. Download this file on to your hard drive in to a place that you will remember. Do not unzip the file. Just save it to your hard drive and login in to your WordPress dashboard.

Once you're logged in, click on "Plugins" and then "Add New" on the menu on the left side.

Above the search option, you'll see some links that say "Search | Upload | Featured..." Click on the link that says "Upload".

Click "Choose File" and locate the .zip file that you just downloaded from the plugin's website. Click the button to open the file and then click "Install Now".

You will see some text appear on the screen followed by "Successfully installed the plugin...". Click "Activate Plugin" and your new plugin will be live and ready.

What plugins do you recommend I start with?

There are literally tens of thousands of plugins available online for WordPress right now. The plugins that are right for your site may not be right for everyone else's site. The functionality that you may want for your site may not be something that everyone else needs.

Saying this, however, there are definitely several plugins that I recommend pretty much every single WordPress website include.

All of the plugins that I'm about to mention can be found by doing the free search inside your WordPress dashboard. These are not premium plugins and you should be able to follow the instructions mentioned earlier to install these.

All In One SEO Pack – This plugin offers "Out-of-the-box SEO" or Search Engine Optimization. Simply installing this plugin will help your blog rank better on sites like Google and Yahoo.

Google XML Sitemaps – This is another search engine

optimization plugin. Installing this plugin will make sure that sites like Google will be able to see and index all of the pages on your website. The more pages Google sees on your website, the easier it is for your website to climb the search engine ranks.

WordPress Database Backup – This is a "peace of mind" plugin. You can set this plugin to back up your WordPress site as often as you like. On some of my more active sites I have it set up to backup daily. On my sites that don't see as much action (less posting / less commenting), I have it set up to backup once per week.

WPtouch – By installing this plugin, you will make sure that your website looks good for people trying to view it on smart phones like iPhones and Androids. People viewing websites via mobile phones is really growing these days. Make sure your site is prepared.

Pretty Link – This plugin is more for people who dabble in affiliate marketing. It allows you to take really ugly affiliate links and make them look like pretty links on your domain. For example, a typical affiliate link may look like "http://demo23.mattrwolfe.hop.clickbank.net/?sid=sidebar1"... By using Pretty Link, I can change that same link to look like "http://myblog.com/wordpress". It looks a lot cleaner.

Subscribe To Comments – This plugin allows people who visit your site and leave a comment to receive and email notification whenever someone replies to their comments. This is great because if they are notified that someone replied to their comment, they will return to your site and continue the conversation. It's great for enticing visitors to return to your site over and over again.

WordPress Popular Posts – This plugin will allow you to add a sidebar widget to your blog's sidebar that displays your most popular posts. This encourages visitors to your site to browse deeper and view more than just the post that they originally came to see.

Sharebar – This plugin is really great for getting people to "Like" your post on Facebook or retweet it on Twitter. It basically adds buttons to Like, Share, Digg, Tweet, etc. to the side of your blog posts. As users scroll down the blog, the sharebar scrolls with them. You can see an example on my blog at BusinessAndBlogs.com.

That's about it for my "must use" plugins for pretty

much all blogs. At one time I would have recommended the Akismet plugin to limit spam as well. However, Akismet has begun charging to use their plugin. It's probably still the best solution out there to reduce spam comments, however, it isn't free. A free plugin called ***Spam Free WordPress*** seems to be a good alternative. However, I haven't done extensive testing with this plugin just yet.

Towards the end of this book, you'll find several interviews that I conducted with some well known bloggers and business owners. These interviews will give you even more insight in to what plugins are available and what various plugins others just couldn't live without.

How many plugins is too many?

The question of how many plugins is too many, really has no answer. Different plugins are different sizes. Some use more memory than others. In some cases, one plugin can be huge and use a ton of memory… in this case, one plugin could already be too much. In other cases, a site can have 100 smaller plugins that use very little memory. There really is no rule of thumb for how many plugins are too many.

If you notice a significant slowdown in your sites performance, it may be a good idea to start scaling back on the plugins.

Another issue that can arise from too many plugins is that some plugins can conflict with each other. Installing a new plugin can cause an old one to stop working. Every time you install a new plugin, test to make sure your site still works the way it once did before continuing to add more plugins.

Content

How do I create an "About Me" page?

To create an "About Me" page with WordPress, simply login to your WordPress dashboard and click on the "Pages" button in the menu on the left side. Click on the "Add New" link to create a new page.

At the top of the screen, where it says "Enter title here", type "About Me".

You can use the large text box on this page to fill in as much or as little detail about yourself as you would like. Use the little buttons along the top of the large text box to add formatting such as bolding and italics, bullet points, and hyperlinks to other websites.

If you want to add a picture of yourself to this page, simply click the link that says "Upload/Insert" above the text box. This will bring up a window where you can drop an image file in.

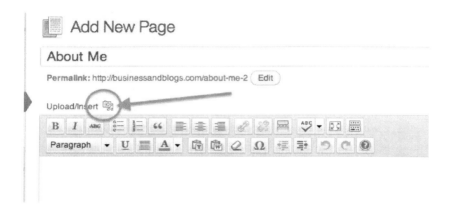

After dropping in the image, you can give the picture a name, a caption, a description, and link it to somewhere else if you would like. Choose how you would like the image aligned. I typically set it as "Left" to make the text appear to the right of the image instead of below the image. Select the image size you'd like to use and then click the button "Insert into Post".

You'll see the image drop in to your large text box.

Maximum upload file size: 7MB. After a file has been uploaded, you can add titles and descriptions.

addimage   Hide

v Page   **File name:** addimage1.jpg

                                File type: image/jpeg

                                Upload date: August 13, 2012

                                Dimensions: 575 × 281

(Edit Image)

Title   *   addimage

Alternate Text

                                Alt text for the image, e.g. "The Mona Lisa"

Caption

Description

Link URL   http://businessandblogs.com/wp-content/uploads/2012/08/addimage1.jpg

                                (None) (File URL) (Attachment Post URL)
                                Enter a link URL or click above for presets.

Alignment   ⦿ ▪ None   ○ ▦ Left   ○ ▦ Center   ○ ▦ Right

Size   ○ Thumbnail *(150 × 150)*
                                ⦿ Medium *(300 × 146)*
                                ○ Large
                                ○ Full Size *(575 × 281)*

                                (Insert into Post)   Use as featured image   Delete

Once your "About Me" page looks the way you want it to, click the button on the left side that says "Publish". You now have an "About Me" page live on your website.

How do I add images to my posts?

Adding an image to a post is the same process that we used to add an image in to our "About Me" page above...

While in your dashboard, click on "Posts" and either add a new post or open an existing post by clicking on the post's name.

Now we're going to click the link that says "Upload/Insert" above the text box. This will bring up a window where you can drop an image file in.

After dropping in the image, you can give the picture a name, a caption, a description, and link it to somewhere else if you would like. Choose how you would like the image aligned. I typically set it as "Left" to make the text appear to the right of the image instead of below the image. Select the image size you'd like to use and then click the button "Insert Into Post". You'll see the image drop in to your large text box.

How do I add videos to my site?

Believe it or not, it's actually extremely simple to add a video to a blog post or page if the video is coming from YouTube. It's really as simple as copying the URL of the video from YouTube and pasting the URL in to your blog post... That's it. WordPress does the rest to make sure the video displays the way it's supposed to display.

Simply go to YouTube and search for the video that you want to share on your blog. Once you are at the video page inside YouTube, grab the link from the top of your browser. It should look something like this: http://www.youtube.com/watch?v=4HAHnWvlaZA. Paste the link in your post. Publish that post once you're done doing any additional writing and click "View Post" to see what it will look like to visitors.

If you're recording a video yourself using screen capture software or your webcam, I recommend using a tool called Easy Video Player (EasyVidPlayer.com). This tool allows you to self-host the videos so that they don't have YouTube branding or YouTube ads in them. It's what I personally use for adding videos to my site to give an extra look of professionalism.

How do I always make sure I have ideas to write about?

One of the toughest things for new bloggers is writer's block. People start their blog and are really excited and have great ideas for the next two weeks worth of posts and then, a month or two passes and they run out of ideas...

I've seen it happen many-a-time... This can be the death of a lot of blogs. If you don't keep the momentum up and you just stop posting, people will move on pretty quickly and it becomes very difficult to rebound and regain that momentum. Don't let this happen to you.

I have several little methods of making sure I never run out of ideas for blog posts.

First of all I use a tool called Evernote that lets me create little lists and notes that I can access from all of my devices. If I make a note on Evernote on my phone, that note shows up on my Mac, my laptop, and my iPad. The notes all sync together. This tool is great for creating lists of blog post ideas wherever you are. Heck, the best idea in the world could come while standing in line at the DMV or while sitting in the bathroom stall at your local Taco Bell... This tool makes it so I always have my blog post idea list with me at all times. Use this tool or something like it (possibly even a pad and paper) to keep an ongoing list of ideas for posts.

For me, the best content for blog posts have been personal experiences. These types of posts may not work in every single niche but they tend to be the easiest for me. I'll run little experiments with my business and then blog about the results, I'll see something in daily life that reminds me of a business concept I can blog about and relate the two, or maybe I'll just share something really cool that happened to me that my readers may be interested in hearing about. These personal posts let people get to know you and are probably the most unique and original content you can write.

Another great way to come up with ideas is to watch the comments on your blog. If you write a great post but people still have a lot of questions, write a follow-up post responding to their questions. Maybe someone asked a question in the comment that requires a long response. Instead of responding in the comments section, write a new blog post with your detailed response. Readers love to know that you're listening.

What are some other effective blog post ideas?

Here's a short list of blog post concepts that have worked extremely well for me.

List posts – List posts are extremely effective, especially if you are making a list of people or websites. For example, I created a list post about the top 10 bloggers than can make you rich. I listed 10 bloggers that taught about online marketing and finance and linked back to their blogs. The people I mentioned were so flattered that they felt compelled to share the post with their followers. The types of posts that stroke the egos of others are excellent because the people you mention want their following to know that others think they are great.

Interviews – Interviews make for real simple and fast content. Simply get on a Skype call with someone that's relevant to your niche and do a 30 minute or hour interview with them. Use a tool like Skype Call Recorder to record the conversation. Take that interview and load it in to Easy Video Player (as a video or an audio) and post it on your page for people to listen to or watch. If you're lucky, the person that you interviewed will share the post with their following as well. A good place to find people to interview is guru.com. If you're running a blog about hypnosis, do a search on guru.com for real hypnotists and contact them for an interview.

Product Reviews – These are easy blog posts as well. Find a product or book that's relevant to your niche and write a review about it. Give a brief overview, list the pros and cons, and tell them whether or not you would recommend it. It's simple, it's effective, and you can probably make a few bucks here and there if you use and affiliate link to the product. Affiliate links and monetization strategies are discussed later.

"How-To" Posts – Create a tutorial on something that you are knowledgeable in. I recommend using pictures so that people can visualize what you're doing. I do these types of posts all the time on how to do various things in WordPress. However, you can do these in any niche. If you're in to gardening, simply take pictures of what you're teaching and use them with your tutorials on your blog.

Case Studies – Similar to how to posts except you are showing somewhat of an experimental process with results from that process. Case studies tend to be more focused on the results of something and less focused on the small details of how to do it.

Those are just a few ideas for blog posts. I'm sure if you use your imagination, you can come up with all sorts of concepts and formulas to keep your blog cranking along.

Traffic

What are your top three sources of traffic?

So you've got your blog online and you have some amazing content written. People should be eating this stuff up because it's so amazing and original. There's only one problem... No one knows about your website.

Nothing seems to slow people's momentum like a website that they put a ton of work in to but no one seems to be visiting and no one seems to care about what you've written. Most people give up pretty quickly when their blog gets no love.

Start of by tackling the following three traffic sources and you'll see visitors slowly start to trickle in. It may not happen overnight, but slowly, you will see visitors and you will begin to pick up momentum.

1. Forum Marketing – This was my absolute largest traffic source when I first started out with my current blog. It is probably the most underrated traffic source but probably the most effective method to see traffic pour in quickly.

With forum marketing, you need to find a forum that is relevant to the niche of your blog. You can usually find some good forums by searching for your niche and "forum" on Google. For example, if I'm in the surfing niche, I would do a search for "surfing forum". Another great place to hunt down forums is called big-boards.com. It's basically a search engine for forums.

Look through these forums for questions that people are asking that you know how to answer. Answer their questions and be as helpful as possible. Use your forum signature to link back to your blog.

When people see how helpful you are on a subject, they will want to learn more from you. If your forum signature has a link back to your blog, it's the natural choice for your new fans to find more info.

2. Blog Commenting – This is very similar to forum marketing except that you are now looking for relevant blogs to comment on. Do a search on Google for your niche plus the word "blog" to find some blogs that are in your niche. For example, a blogger who blogs about model planes would search "Model Plane Blog" and see what comes up.

Once you've found some relevant blogs, read the blog posts and join the conversation in the comments below the post. Share what you thought about the post, mention ideas that the writer may have left out, or even answer questions that others have asked in the comments. Be sure to leave the URL for your blog in the correct box and watch as other readers of that blog as well as the blogger themselves start checking out your blog to see what you're contributing.

Make sure that when you start commenting on blogs that you avoid promoting your own blog. Unless you have a blog post that's really relevant to the post you're commenting on, you'll probably upset both the blogger and their readers and possibly even be flagged as spam. Just putting the link to your blog in the URL box in the comments section should be enough to see traffic. So be helpful and thoughtful, without over-promotion, and you'll find that blog commenting can result in some pretty good traffic.

3. Social Media – This traffic source is actually very general because social media really encompasses a ton of different traffic sources. You've got Facebook, Twitter, LinkedIn, YouTube, Google Plus, and on and on and on.

What I typically recommend is to pick two of your favorite social media platforms and focus on those. For me, I've had the most success generating traffic through Facebook and through YouTube.

With Facebook, I simply make sure that I share any new posts that I make on my blog with my followers. I specifically ask them to leave comments and feedback. I purposely do not use automated software to do this either because I like to leave my own comments and extra info when posting. Automating these types of posts to Facebook tends to cause a lot of people to ignore and skip over them.

With YouTube, I like to create videos that teach something helpful in my niche. I then put the link back to my blog directly below my video as well as make sure to give a call to action in my video. For example, at the end of my video I might say, "Don't forget to check out my blog for more tips by clicking the link directly below this video."

For some people, creating videos and putting them on

YouTube is a nerve-wracking and uncomfortable experience. If that's the case, play around with Twitter or Google Plus and see if you can make those work for you. If something seems to work well for creating traffic to your site, by all means, stick with it.

How do you build a list with WordPress?

Probably the most powerful tool anyone doing business online has is their mailing list. With a mailing list you can ask people who have visited your site already to come back over and over again. Simply do an email broadcast, telling your list about your latest blog post, and watch as your followers flood back to your site to read your latest post and share their feedback.

Creating a mailing list with WordPress requires an extra tool that has a small monthly cost attached to it. You need something called an auto responder which costs about $20 per month when you first get started. The cost is totally worth it though once you build this invaluable asset over time.

An auto responder is the tool that you use to collect the email addresses. The monthly cost is the fee for storing these email addresses and for having the ability to blast out email messages to the whole list at will. You can even set up automated emails that go out to your list in set intervals. For example, when someone signs up to your list, you can have the auto responder immediately send out an email thanking them for joining and giving them a link to a cool resource. Two days after subscribing, the system can send out another message with a link to an older blog post that you think the readers may enjoy. You can completely automate your email marketing.

The auto responder service I use and recommend is called Aweber and can be found at Aweber.com. They are pretty much universally recognized as the best in the industry and you can't go wrong with them. In fact, I believe it's only $1 for the first month to get started with them.

Now, to actually build this mailing list, you need to do a couple of things.

First I recommend offering some sort of freebie to entice visitors of your blog to give you their email address. Create a one or two page report about your area of expertise and offer this in exchange for signing up. You can have your auto responder message immediately deliver the freebie upon sign up to keep things as automated as possible.

Second, you need to put an opt-in form somewhere on your blog. There are many ways of putting an opt-in form on your blog and the one you use is really up to personal taste.

Many people put the opt-in form in their sidebar inside of a text widget. To do this, you simply need to take the code that Aweber gives you and put it inside of a text widget in the widgets area of your dashboard. You can review how to add a widget to your WordPress site in the "What is a widget?" section.

Others like to use a lightbox on their blog. A lightbox is similar to a pop-up. Once someone lands on your blog a box pops up in front of the content asking the reader to give their email address in exchange for a bonus. Many people feel this is a bit intrusive and ruins the experience of visiting your site. If you do go this route, I recommend using a plugin called Popup Domination (popupdom.com). It makes beautiful looking lightboxes. It's probably the most effective way to build a list, however, be ready for people to not be a huge fan of the technique.

Finally, the way I like to collect opt-ins is via an opt-in box at the bottom of my blog posts. The reason I put the opt-in at the bottom of my posts is because I only get the highest quality opt-ins. I only get people that decided to give me their email AFTER reading one of my posts. If they're giving me their email, they must have liked what I had to say and want to hear from me more. This builds the list a lot slower but makes for a very responsive following. I recommend a premium plugin for this called Optin Skin to make beautiful, below-post, opt-in boxes.

How do you leverage Facebook for traffic?

Other than simply making sure you keep your Facebook following updated with your latest posts, there are many other ways to leverage Facebook with your blog.

When people "like" one of your blog posts on Facebook, their whole following sees that they "liked" the post. Because of this, it's to your benefit to try and get as many "likes" as possible on every single one of your blog posts.

Earlier on, I mentioned a plugin called Sharebar. I love this plugin for encouraging people to "Like" a post. The "Like" button floats down the page with them as they read your post, giving them the ability to click it and share the love at any point.

For me, simply sharing my posts on Facebook once they are made, asking people to like my posts and re-share them, adding the sharebar to my blog, and then just being really active on Facebook seems to do the trick for getting loads of visitors.

I do think it is key to be really active on Facebook. The more people that you interact with frequently, the more people you'll see pay attention when you post something. Don't always post business related things either. This is probably the biggest mistake I see most site owners do. They post only links to blog posts and nothing else and everyone seems to ignore them...

Be a real person on Facebook. Talk about vacations, hanging out with a good friend, going to the water park, and so on. People love seeing the personal side of the experts that they follow. It helps them connect with you more and get to know you as a real person. Pull the human element out of it and it's a guaranteed way to see no love from Facebook.

Monetization

What are some ways to make money from my blog?

There are so many different ways that you can make money with your blog. Some are more difficult and take quite a bit more effort while some can be done with just a few clicks. As a general rule of thumb, expect to make more money off the difficult ones that take time and be ready to wait on the easier ones.

Adsense Ads – Adsense is probably the most simple way to start making money with your blog. You basically set up an account with Google Adsense and they will give you a little snippet of code which you can simply paste in to the sidebar of your blog. Google's algorithm's will attempt to find relevant ads and place them inside your sidebar for you.

There are definitely pros and cons to Adsense. Of course it's very simple and fast to set up but expect to make spare change with your ads. Even some of my highly trafficked sites only made a few dollars per month in some cases.

For some reason, Adsense seems to work extremely well for some niches and not at all for others. For example, Adsense does not seem to have good results in business or marketing related niches. Even though Business and Blogs receives a lot of traffic every month, I wouldn't put Adsense on it because it's just not very profitable. On the other hand, I have a health niche website with Adsense on it that makes upwards of $200 per month from the ads. So it's definitely worth a test in your niche.

To set up Adsense on your blog, simply navigate to Adsense.com and create an account. If you already have an account with Google, you should be able to use your existing login details.

Once logged in to Adsense, you can click on the "My ads" tab at the top of the screen and then the "New ad unit" button on the page that follows.

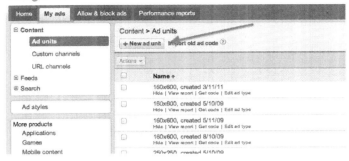

Name your ad and choose a size. Since we're putting this in the sidebar of our blog, I recommend using a skyscraper style banner that's taller than it is wide. Leave your "Ad type" as "Text & image/rich media ads" and then select an ad style at the bottom where the colors best match your existing WordPress theme. Click "Save and get code". Copy the code that Adsense gives you on the next page and you're ready to place the ad on your blog.

Log in to your WordPress dashboard and click on the "Appearance" link and then the "Widgets" link in your left sidebar. Drag a Text widget in to your sidebar. Paste the code that Adsense just gave you inside that text widget and click "Save".

Jump over to your website's URL and take a look at your new site with the Adsense banner in place. Please note that the first time you install an Adsense banner, it could take up to several hours for ads to start displaying in that spot. So if you do see a blank area where the ads should be, don't be discouraged. It may take a little bit of time.

Affiliate Marketing – Promoting other people's products through affiliate marketing is another great way to monetize your blog and is actually one of the two main ways that I make money from Business and Blogs right now.

Basically, with affiliate marketing, you are promoting products and programs that other people created that are relevant to your website and making a commission on the sales of those products.

There are some really great reasons why I love affiliate marketing as a monetization strategy but there are definitely some pitfalls of making it your only strategy.

Personally, I love it because I don't have to create the products. Someone does 90% of the work on a product and usually gives me 50% of the sales price for simply mentioning it. I also love affiliate marketing because the product creator handles customer support. If there are issues with the program or product, the tech support is almost entirely handled by someone else. Gotta love that.

The main problem with affiliate marketing is that it is very difficult to have much success with it before you build up a following. If your blog doesn't have many visitors and you have yet to grow your mailing list, you may struggle to see early results from affiliate marketing.

Some ways that I like to use affiliate marketing are through banner ads (see the sidebar on businessandblogs.com). I simply put up little ads for the products that I recommend. I occasionally get clicks on these products which sometimes lead to sales. But over time banner ads have been used so much that people actually become "ad blind". They simply don't pay attention to the ads anymore. This makes sales via banner ads very slow.

I also like to do product reviews. I'll use my blog to list of the pros and cons of a particular product and then use my affiliate link for the readers to purchase it based on my review.

This works really well as long as you do a good job of proving that you are being unbiased with the review. Make sure to list both pros AND cons with a product. If every product review you ever do describes the best product on earth, your reviews will start to lose their credibility.

Finally, I'm a fan of doing product demos. These are like product reviews but instead I give the user an inside look of a product. If I'm trying to get them to purchase Easy Video Player, for example, I might create a video where I log in to my Easy Video Player account and show them all the features and go through the steps of setting up a video with it. These inside looks really make the readers feel comfortable with the product. When they see what they're going to get before they get it from a resource they trust, it makes it much easier to sell them on the product.

Of course the absolute best way to make money through affiliate marketing is to build up that list that we started building in an earlier chapter, and market your review posts and your product demos to that list... So I can never stress enough how important it is to get that list built as fast as possible. Don't skip that step!

Product Creation – Creating my own products has been the absolute secret to my success thus far. Every time I learn how to do something really cool in the online marketing world I like to turn around and make a video training product out of it. This was how the WordPress Classroom initially started... I learned how to blog then turned around and taught others.

Creating my own products and then selling them through my mailing list and through my blog has made me my living for the past three years. It's paid my mortgage payment and allowed my wife to leave her job so that we can start a family. It's also the only way you're probably going to build a mailing list of buyers, and buyers are the highest quality subscribers.

Products can come in many forms. You can write eBooks, you can create videos, you can record audios, you can do live training on webinars or you can do live events in person. It's up to you decide what type of product is right for you. I will tell you this however; the further outside of your comfort zone the product is to create, the more money it probably stands to make you.

EBooks are easy to make. You can use MS Word or a free word processor like Open Office and save the report as a

PDF. However, eBooks are becoming harder and harder to sell. With internet connections only getting faster, people prefer to learn through video or through live interaction. EBooks have almost gotten to a point where people expect them to be free. Therefore, it's become more difficult to get good money for your training eBook.

Recording a video, on the other hand, tends to make people uncomfortable. People are afraid to get on camera or even just have their voice on camera. However, it's much easier to sell training via video because there is less doubt in the consumers' minds that what you're teaching is possible... They are seeing it happen in front of them on camera. It's less likely that what you're teaching isn't going to work. Videos just sell better.

Offer Services – The final monetization strategy that I'm going to discuss is the idea that you can actually sell services to your readers. This has the potential to be the most profitable option out of all of them.

You can offer consulting on your niche. With your blog, you'll be considered an expert in your niche. People will read your stuff and consider you an authority. Being a leading authority on a subject means that you can consult with people who are also trying to get in to your niche. You can sell your expertise for top dollar once you start to build that credibility and that reputation through your blog.

You can also offer done-for-you services from your blog. This may be more relevant in computer related niches but I'm sure there are creative people out there that can figure out how to do this in their niche. For example, with WordPress, I offer the services of setting up sites for people. I'll do as little as just getting the site installed all the way up to custom designing a site with a fully functioning membership aspect. I'm willing to do any of it. Just be prepared because I'm not cheap.

Being the credible authority in your niche allows you to charge top dollar for your services and your time. Don't be afraid to create a WordPress page with your contact details and the services you offer. You may be shocked at how often people are willing to pay the expert in their niche to just take care of it for them. It can be a really great profit center.

Miscellaneous Questions

What is an RSS feed?

RSS stands for Real Simple Syndication. It's a way for your followers to keep up to date with your blog posts through RSS readers as well as a way for other sites to automatically pull the content out of your site and post it elsewhere.

Many people who like to read blogs often prefer to read all of their favorite blogs from one place without having to go to every single site every day to find out if it's been updated. With an RSS reader like Google reader, people can view all of their favorite posts from within the reader. The reader will keep them up to date with new posts from their favorite blogs.

Many people like to use their RSS feed to syndicate their blog's content on other sites as well. For example, in Facebook, you can actually add an RSS feed to a Facebook page and every time you add a new post to your blog, Facebook will pull the blog post from your RSS feed and post it to Facebook. It's a way to not have to repost the same content in multiple places.

How do I set up my RSS feed?

By using WordPress, you automatically have an RSS feed. It's something that's built in and works right out of the box. However, the built in RSS feature isn't really that great... You can't see stats of how many people are following you, you can't control how much content is displayed in the feed, and, if you ever change your domain name, your RSS feed won't come with you.

There's a better way to do RSS...

If you go to http://feedburner.com, you can use Google's service for managing RSS feeds. With Feedburner, you can watch how many subscribers your blog's feed has, manage how much content is shown, move your site to different domain names while keeping your subscribers, place ads in your feed, and much much more.

Simply go to http://feedburner.com, login with your Google account details, enter the URL of your blog in the text box on the screen, and click the "Next" button. You'll have a feedburner RSS feed ready in minutes.

Once you've done those steps, Feedburner will give you a URL that looks something like feeds.feedburner.com/your-blog-name/... This will be your RSS feed URL.

Login to your WordPress dashboard, go to the section to add a new plugin, and search for "FD Feedburner". Install and activate the FD Feedburner plugin. Go to the settings for this plugin and set the URL to the feeds.feedburner.com URL that Feedburner just gave you.

Now you've got an optimized RSS feed setup and you're ready to go. The people that prefer to read blogs through RSS feeds can now do so and you can now track your feed stats at Feedburner.com.

How do I customize my menu?

Recently, the creators of WordPress made it simple to customize menus on your website. By default, WordPress takes every page that you create and puts it in your header menu (if your theme has a header menu). A lot of people don't want every single page that they create to show up in that menu. If you're one of those people, you're going to want to set up a custom menu.

To set up a custom menu, simply login to your dashboard, click "Appearance" in the menu on the left, then click on "Menus".

At the top of the screen, enter a name for your menu. I usually just call mine "Main Menu". Once you've named it click "Create Menu".

You will now see some boxes on the left side with "Theme Locations", "Custom Links", "Pages", and "Categories"...

Under "Theme Locations", use the drop down menu below "Primary Menu" to select the "Main Menu" you just created and click "Save".

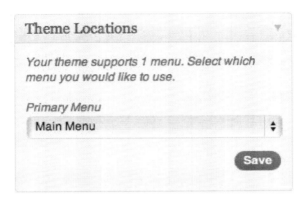

You can now select the pages that you want to include in your top menu and click the button that says "Add to Menu". You can also add custom links to your top menu if you'd like by filling in the details in the "Custom Links" box.

Once you've added some pages and some links to your menu, you can reorganize your menu by dragging the various boxes around on the right side. Order them in the way that you want them to appear in your header and click "Save Menu" when you are done. The menu will not show up properly unless you click "Save Menu" when you are done.

That's all there is to it. You now have complete control over how your menu looks and acts on your website.

How do I add "Read More" to my post?

Many people want to have just little snippets of their blog posts appear on the main home page with a button that says "Read More" after the snippet. This makes their home page look like much less text and just gives a bit of a teaser for each post.

This is actually really simple to do. When you're creating a new blog post, type the portion of the post that you want to be the snippet before it cuts off. Immediately after the teaser content section, click on the button in your post editor that looks like two rectangles with a dotted line between them. This will add a break and a "Read More" button to the post. It will also add a visual line inside the text editor. Everything above the line will show on your main homepage. Everything below the line will be shown after they click in to read the whole post.

How do I schedule a post for later?

Have you ever had several good ideas for blog posts but didn't want to post them all at once right after the other? This is a good scenario to schedule a post for later so that you can write multiple posts now and have them show up at future dates and times.

To do this, create a new blog post. Once you're finished with your blog post, look for the "Publish" box on the right side of the screen. You'll see some text that says "Publish Immediately". Click on the "Edit" button located directly to the right of "Publish Immediately". This will bring up a box to set the date and time that you want this blog post to go live.

Pick your date and time and press "Ok". The big blue "Publish" button will change to a big blue "Schedule" button. Click "Schedule" and your post will be queued to go live on the specified date and time.

How do I make sure my site is secure from hackers?

Many people are constantly asking me about securing their website. It really seems to be a growing concern. With a few precautionary measures, you should have a pretty safe blog. WordPress's security is pretty reliable right out of the box.

Although prevention is the best method, I highly recommend that you install the WordPress Database Backup plugin that we mentioned in the plugins section of this book. That way, even if all your best efforts fail, you'll be able to restore your blog back to normal in no time at all.

Some measures that I recommend taking to make sure your site is as secure as possible would be to start off by picking a good username and password. Don't use the default "Admin" username. Pick a unique login username that's not simple to guess. Pick a good password as well. Avoid common passwords like "password" and "abc123". Use a difficult password to guess and include numbers and even characters like exclamation marks or question marks.

Make sure that you update WordPress whenever there's a new update available. Most WordPress updates include security updates. One of the main reasons it seems like there are constantly new versions is because the creators are constantly searching for security holes and fixing them. Keeping your WordPress installation up to date is vital to making sure you've got the latest security features installed.

If you're still worried about security, you can install a

free plugin called WP Login Lock. This plugin will ban people from logging in if they try and fail several times. It will also force you to reset your password every so often as an added measure of safety.

Following these few simple steps, you shouldn't have any issues with people trying to hack your site.

How do I upgrade WordPress?

WordPress constantly has new upgrades to fix little bugs and security holes. It's important that you update whenever possible.

You will know when a new update is available because when you login to your dashboard you'll see a message that says something like "WordPress 3.4.1 is available! Please update now" at the top of the screen. When you see that message, simply click on the "Please update now" link and click on the button that says "Update Automatically".

WordPress will recommend that you backup your database before upgrading. Luckily, if you've followed along, you've already got a backup because you're using WP Database backup.

Bonus Expert Interviews

As an added bonus, I chased up some of the leading experts in marketing and blogging on the internet and gave them a few quick interview questions. I asked them to talk to me a little bit about what they use WordPress for, what plugins they could not live without, how they make money with WordPress, and what piece of advice they would give to beginners.

If there's any part of this book that you should absolutely pay attention to, it's this section. This is where I personally learned the most while creating this book. I talked to people that are in the trenches, making WordPress work for them.

Pay close attention to the variety of plugins that people use as well as the plugins that everyone seems to have in common. Also pay attention to the wide variety of ways that people actually monetize their blogs. The information contained in this interview section is easily worth four times the cost of this book. So dog-ear it, highlight it, bookmark it, and do whatever else is necessary to make sure you remember what these experts have to share with you because this part is pure gold.

Some of our experts went in to real great detail with their answers and some went for bare bones. Either way, these are some great insights in to what you can do with WordPress and how some of the most successful people I know are making it work for them.

Sean Vossler

www.sean.co

What do you use WordPress for?

I've been working with WordPress for many years, and my uses have changed much over time. I started out hand coding websites as a high school kid, and loved building them, but it's obviously not an ideal way to develop a lot of dynamic websites. I found out about WordPress and after many hours fussing with a $5 GoDaddy server I got it up and running. After college I started my own small web design company, and quit my day job. I basically built the business completely around WordPress and my graphic design skills.

After a few years and about 70 websites I slowed my web design business and moved more into the online marketing sphere, there I was able to use my WordPress skills extensively. First building out landing pages for products, and then developing membership websites to house the content for those products.

Now I'm mainly focused on product development

around WordPress as a platform for business. My latest project helps business owners learn WordPress and membership plugins to help them develop continuity programs for their business. It's a real joy to use a platform that is always improving, and always has the users in mind.

What are the absolute essential plugins that you couldn't live without?

Digg Digg - Social Media Buttons

WishList - Memberships

CodeCanyon.net (not a plugin, but a lot of unique plugins on this site)

Advanced Category Widget - Great widget for blogs

Easy Content Types - Take WP Custom Posts to the next level

Intense Debate - Comment system, great for ranking comments

Pipity - Pop up domination alternative

Quick Page/Post Redirection - Set up redirects (ex. sean.co/wp)

WP-Cache - Simple, effective cache plugin

What's your favorite way to monetize a WordPress website?

I've tried a LOT of different ways, and many of them work quite well. When talking about monetization you have to consider traffic first, without traffic you have nothing to monazite on. In my experience, a good goal for monetization is to have your site cover one of your basic bills, like car bill or mortgage. Say it's $500 a month; next you need to calculate your CPM (income per 1000 visitors) for your site and for your minimization method. This can get pretty complex, but say you make $10 off ads for every 1000 visitors, then to reach your $500 goal you need to generate 50,000 views on your site per month.

My favorite method for monetizing a website is to view it as a business. Develop a business model around your site or blog, and pick the right monetization method for that business. One of the most effective is the 'list building' method, where you don't try and get them to click on an ad or buy a product, you get your visitor to opt into an email list. From there you can send targeted email messages and offers to your visitors over email- a surprisingly effective method especially if you have low traffic on your site. Figures very, but you can build a six figure business around a list of around 10,000 responsive emails, if done correctly.

Monetization in order of difficulty (to me):
Advertising (banners/text)

Affiliate marketing integration (Amazon / Clickbank)

List building

Continuity Programs (membership website)

Selling Your Website

What's the best piece of advice you can give to someone getting started with WordPress?

Never loose site that if you're looking to use WordPress for business that it's simply a platform. You'll need people to help you get to the next level, keep networking with key people in your industry. Once you have WordPress as a skill in your toolbox, use it to help others... The law of reciprocity is an amazing thing.

Glen Allsopp

www.ViperChill.com

www.OptinSkin.com

What do you use WordPress for?

I use Wordpress as the platform to share my message. More often than not, this is through words on blog posts, but I also utilize the pages to send people to other resources I've created like my tutorial videos or the podcast episodes that I've been involved in.

Additionally, I use it as the backbone of our software company, which creates plugins specifically for the CMS.

What are the absolute essential plugins that you couldn't live without?

Align RSS Images is a big one, since it allows images to be properly formatted in your RSS feed (I'm amazed Wordpress doesn't use this by default).

FX Gravatar Cache is another biggie, since Gravatar

images in comments can drastically slow down your blog -- especially if you get hundreds of comments like some of our posts. It saves Gravatar images in your server cache, rather than constantly requesting them from Gravatar.com

I couldn't live without *OptinSkin.com* either, but obviously I'm biased.

Finally, I would say any kind of caching plugin is essential, since the speed of your site has a dramatic effect on whether people stick around, subscribe, and / or buy your products. *W3 Cache* and *WPSupercache* are good for this.

What's your favorite way to monetize a WordPress website?

I only sell software, so that's probably the main one. Having an audience who read your regular content updates also makes it possible to make a good income as an affiliate, but that depends on your niche.

What's the best piece of advice you can give to someone getting started with WordPress?

Don't worry about getting everything perfect before you

take action. If you're serious about building a popular blog, spend as much time as you can on your design though as you can. It's importance should not be understated. You can see within a few seconds whether someone cares about their site from its design. You can figure out what your audience likes and how to create killer posts as time goes on.

Ori Bengal

www.CouchSurfingOri.com

www.MakeWpEasy.com

What do you use WordPress for?

Wordpress is so darn flexible. I've used it for my personal blog (covering marketing, creativity, and my adventures)- which has really built up my personal brand.

I've used it to make a site to help my brother adopt a child.

I've used it to make a website for my parents' business, as well as many clients' websites.

I've used it to make an online course (which is a membership site) which keeps making money, so that I can work on the things I'm passionate about (like drawing, and capoeira).

I've used it to make a website to raise $1,500 for a 1 year old poodle that belonged to some student that had no money, and needed $1,500 for a procedure for said Poodle... or he'd die.

It's just such a flexible tool, I could go on for hours about the uses.

What are the absolute essential plugins that you couldn't live without?

Akismet - Spam is evil

Gravity Forms - By far my favorite form plugin

BackWpUp - It's free and it backs my site up to multiple places in the cloud

Redirection - Lets me mask links as couchsurfingori.com/blah-blah - which is fantastic for affiliate linking.

CMS Page Tree View - You know... this one is definitely in the can't live without category. It is how Wordpress should natively show their page layout.

What's your favorite way to monetize a WordPress website?

I dislike PPC ads. I know you asked about what my favorite is... but I think what I dislike is important as well. Here's why: They look cheesy, you only get paid a tiny bit for each click, and you're sending the traffic away from your site.

What I do like is affiliate links (and I make sure to make them open up in a new browser), getting people to opt-in, so I can communicate with them, and sometimes promote to them...

Then there's the video sales letters -- sites that are used to just sell a product or service. And affiliates drive traffic to it for me.

What's the best piece of advice you can give to someone getting started with WordPress?

You don't need to know everything. It's like Photoshop-- everyone asks me how to learn it. Well.. there's a zillion uses, a zillion buttons, and a zillion plugins. So.. don't try to "Learn Wordpress" -- figure out what you want it to do, and learn that.

Again, I'll use Photoshop as a metaphor -- I can create beautiful text in Photoshop, or I can fix the lens distortion, or I can get rid of a zit in a photo, or I can bring out detail that wasn't there, or I can (and do) create beautiful paintings, or I can design a website, or I can lay out an ad or magazine page. Each one would involve a different tutorial.

Wordpress is the same -- whether you want to secure it, back it up, make it faster, make it prettier, make your own themes, make a new marketing trick, make an ecommerce site, make a membership site, make a portfolio site... these things are all different-- and you don't need to know them all to get started.

Use Google, check out my course or Matt's course, get on various forums or FB groups.... It's so easy these days to get instant answers.

The bottom line is, don't get overwhelmed. This stuff is easy -- it may be frustrating at first, 'cause it's new... but it's easy, and once you solve a problem, you learn how to recognize it.

Also, delegate. You CAN create your own themes. You CAN program your own plugins... I just don't know why you would. There is so much technical work that goes into it, and there are already countless people making all that stuff for you. So... rather than investing your energy and time in that, just find what's out there that works, and customize that to your needs.

Lastly, and I guess just phrasing things a bit differently -

- you gotta understand WHY people think that websites are really difficult, and thus expensive.... It is because in the 90's, we had to make everything by hand. Every page was coded from scratch. We had to know HTML. CSS didn't even exist, so the menus had to be created on every single page of your site. There were no stock-photography websites, and so we had to spend so much time on everything. God forbid a change should be needed.

You really did need your web designer to make any change for you. These days however, you install Wordpress with the push of a button, you upload your theme that you paid $40 for, you install a bunch of plugins that were free, and you spend $20 on top-notch images. Boom! 1 day, and you have a website that looks 1,000 times better than any site in the 90's ever did, and has so much power.

Want to make a change? Log in, push a button. Done!

The only reason people think this is hard is because 20 years ago, it really was... and because web designers want you to think it's hard, or they can't charge you as much.

Dive in, and have fun! It really is fun. Oh yeah... adding

to question #2 -- What do I use Wordpress for? I use it on the
barter system. You can get just about anything you want or need
in exchange for a good website.

Casey Zeman

www.CaseyZemanOnline.com

www.YoutubeRevealed.com

www.EasyWebinarPlugin.com

What do you use WordPress for?

For creating blogs, membership sites, creating automated webinars, and building fast and easy web pages.

What are the absolute essential plugins that you couldn't live without?

Wishlist – To create membership sites

W3 Total Cache – To make my site load faster

Google Sitemap – To help with search engine optimization

Video Sitemap – To help optimize my videos for the search engines

All-In-One SEO – To better optimize my site for search engines

Popup Domination – To build my mailing list with popups

Easy Webinar Plugin – To run automated webinars on WordPress

Digg-Digg – Similar to Sharebar – To encourage social sharing on my site

Redirection – Redirects any dead pages to a page of my choice

What's your favorite way to monetize a WordPress website?

I mostly monetize WordPress with my membership site, sales pages, and through webinars with Easy Webinar Plugin.

What's the best piece of advice you can give to someone getting started with WordPress?

Wordpress is the easiest way to create a real dynamic site that you can Control YOURSELF. The trouble with getting developers and designers and webmasters is that you are always held by their timeline. With Wordpress, you can get in there create new content, structure the pages the way you want. You have the control!

Christina Hills

www.websitecreationworkshop.com

What do you use WordPress for?

I use WordPress for my own websites and I teach people how to build their own WordPress sites.

What are the absolute essential plugins that you couldn't live without?

The *quick page post redirect* plugin
The *duplicate post plugin*
The *all in one seo* pack
The *Shareaholic* social media plugin
The *Backup Buddy* Plugin for backing up and moving websites

What's your favorite way to monetize a WordPress website?
My favorite way to monetize a WordPress website is to sell my own training programs

What's the best piece of advice you can give to someone getting started with WordPress?

If you are just starting out with WordPress, and you are not a 'techie' person then you should pick a simple theme like 2010 to learn WordPress on, until you get comfortable with it.

Then you should move to a more elaborate theme. (You can find a great collection of themes at TheBestThemes.com)

This will make learning the basics easier.

Also, don't try to learn everything all at once! WordPress can be very complicated, so just stick to creating your content with posts and pages. Creating content is the most important thing to do with WordPress!

Pat Flynn

www.SmartPassiveIncome.com

A quick explanation...

The following is parts of a transcript from an older audio interview that I did with Pat Flynn of Smart Passive income. Because these were taken from an older audio interview (before I ever intended to write this book), the questions asked are slightly different than the questions that I asked the other experts and the answers are very in-depth and in more of a conversational tone. There are some real gold nuggets in this interview and Pat really holds nothing back. Enjoy!

Can you give us a little bit about your back story and kind of how you got into blogging? What you did before you were doing this stuff?

I went to college for architecture at UC Berkeley. I loved the field. I was really interested in it. I got a great job after graduating and I thought that's what I was going to do for the rest of my life. I'm different from the people who make money online now who say things like *"oh I hated my 9 to 5 job and I just want to go find something different"*. I actually loved my job and they kind of kicked me out when the US economy tanked in 2008...

It was a really tough time for me because I had just gotten engaged and I was supposed to start a family soon. I was kind of struggling in my own head for a couple of weeks as far as what I was going to do. I actually did look for another job in the architectural industry and it was just impossible. No one was building anything so nobody needed me to design any buildings.

I was really looking for some help, but luckily, while I was still working – just kind of backtracking a little bit – I actually started a blog for this exam I was taking called *The LEED Exam*, which stands for Leadership Energy and Environmental Designs.

The reason I created this blog was to help me keep track of my notes. I did a lot of traveling and it was a lot easier for me to study by posting notes on a blog and then reading them back later. I was working through the content management system, WordPress which allowed me to share my notes online with my coworkers. I really had no intention of ever showing it to anyone else but then I got laid off.

I had passed the exam a few months before I was laid off and I just let the little site sit there. I didn't really plan on doing anything with it, but then I got interested in internet marketing. There was a podcast I was listening to and some blogs that I was reading that really inspired me. Everybody was telling me that the internet was a great place to potentially make a living and do good things online. So one of the first things I did was I took this blog that I had already made and I decided to share it with other people. The next day I actually put an analytical plugin on the site and found that for the last six months, people were already visiting that site...

It kind of just blew me away. Literally 5,000 to 6,000 visitors a day, which was kind of crazy. At first I kind of got startled and scared. I didn't know if what I was doing was legal. I was worried that maybe the notes weren't good enough for people to pass the exam. But then I flipped the switch a little bit and thought, *"okay well maybe I can actually become a resource for people who are interested in this. I took it, I know how it works, I passed it and it went really well. Maybe I can help others"*. So that's kind of the path that I took after that.

I started to revamp the site, come back to the site every day and make it better, help people out, and introduce new tips. It became kind of a top resource in that industry. People shared it with more people. I was getting up to 8,000 or 9,000 visitors a day at that point.

I started to want to monetize the blog. The first thing that I learned from reading blogs and listening to podcasts was to add AdSense on the site. I tried that and, the first day, I made about $5 which was great. I just put up some code and immediately I had $5 which is like lunch, but it was a great start. It showed me that this was actually possible.

So the next thing I did was I introduced private advertising. I rented out some space on the site for advertising. I actually emailed and phoned other companies to see if they wanted to get some of the traffic that my site was getting. Many of them agreed. I was now making maybe $300 to $600 per month off of private advertising and AdSense combined after a couple of months.

The site had already been up for about a year and a half. It already had a following which takes a while to build up. I just want to make sure to let people know this before they think this is like a get-rich-quick thing.

After seeing a little success, I joined what's called a Mastermind Group. I found other people in my area who were really into the internet business, some who were just starting, some who were already making a lot of money.

One person in the group, who was more knowledgeable than I was, suggested that I write an eBook for the site... I was like, *"okay well what's an eBook?"*. He showed me that it's an electronic book like a PDF that you can sell on your site. It's somewhat automated so that people can come to your site, they can buy the book, and it automatically gets delivered to them. Now I was like, *"this sounds really cool but it's going to take a lot of work. I don't know if it's the right thing to do. What am I going to put in the book? Everything that I would include is already free on the site."* But he said, *"No trust me. What have you got to lose?"* So I did it and, about 10 minutes later, I had a completed PDF file done to sell as an eBook.

The first month I sold it, October of 2008, I made $7,905.83 or something like that... almost $8000 dollars. It was totally life changing for me and it was even more incredible because I was actually helping people. When I tell people I do business online, they usually think I'm doing something like porno or something that I shouldn't be doing. But I'm actually, legitimately, providing information for people who want to pay me back in return, which is great.

So I was making $8,000 dollars and then I introduced an audio guide along with it and it went to $14,000, $16,000, $21,000 all the way up to $30,000 dollars in a single month for just a few hours per week answering customer emails. The business was automated. Because it was an electronic product, I didn't have to go to the post office and send anything.

When I got married, things were just fantastic. That's when I really changed gears with a blog I created called Smart Passive Income. This is the site that most people know me from.

Smart Passive Income was originally created to talk about how I was starting to make money off of AdSense and things like that. Right before I got laid off, I was really thinking of new ways to make money because I knew that I was about to get laid off. I started Smart Passive Income when things started to really takeoff with the eBook. I just wanted to share with other people that this is really happening. I just wanted to be honest for a month and show people exactly what I did, what I did wrong, what I would have done better.

Since then I've been creating new businesses online... More niche sites, more affiliate marketing, iPhone applications, article writing, all these types of things, showing people exactly the step-by-step process that I've taken and what I've done wrong. I know there's people out there who want to do the same thing and I'm hopefully providing an honest, non-hyped up way to view everything... and showing people what I did wrong to hopefully help them do it the right way the first time. I now have a podcast for the Smart Passive Income Blog. I have a thriving YouTube channel, a Facebook page and 15,000 Twitter followers.

It's just been an incredible journey. I'm always trying to give back and help people through email because the more people I can help, the more karma pays me back.

What is the optimal schedule for making blog posts?

It's going to be different for everybody because I know Glenn Allsopp (ViperChill.com) posts once a month and that's good enough for him. Me, I post three times a week and that's good for me. That's what I found to be comfortable. Some people do once a week. As long as the content is there and you're providing what your audience needs then it doesn't really matter as long as you're consistent. If I were to do once a month one month and then every day the next month it would confuse everybody. It would confuse me as a writer too. If you're just starting out it might take awhile to find your groove but, once you find your groove, stick to it.

Sometimes you create a schedule and then it's time for you write a blog post and it's not always easy. If you feel like sometimes you have to force it out, being flexible with your topics and being able to do content in different platforms helps. Maybe I just can't write that day but I can record an audio, or shoot a video instead. That helps me keep going when, if I was just on one platform, I wouldn't be able to.

How do you constantly come up with new ideas for content?

A lot of what I write about is based on the businesses that I'm running and those businesses change all the time. Those businesses are being improved on all the time and being tested all the time. So it's really easy for me to just write content about that and people are interested in it. It becomes all about the numbers and the results and the split tests and studying and that type of thing.

I did something called the niche site dual which was following the progress of a site from start to finish and that's what the content was. It was really easy for me to figure out what it was about because it was just what was happening at that time so I was just reporting on it.

Other times, I'll write a post that other people had asked me to write. One tip is, if you have an auto responder, is to engage with people. Not a lot of people do that. So one thing I'll actually do is I'll ask in the fourth or fifth email... I send an email saying *"Hey thank you so much for being on the list. I want to ask you is there anything that you'd like me to write about on the blog?"* This constantly gives me new ideas from readers about what to write about.

So I don't even have to think about it at that point. I may get *"Hey I need help with figuring out how to optimize my YouTube videos for SEO."*... If I get that question two or three times I just put that in the queue for potential blog post ideas.

Sometimes I'll just ask on Facebook. Facebook is amazing, as far as the community is concerned, with figuring out what they want. The thing is that is who my audience is so they're telling me exactly what my audience wants to see instead of me coming up with something that may or may not be an interest to people.

What are the absolute essential plugins that you couldn't live without?

One of them is called *Pretty Link* it shortens your huge affiliate links from places like Amazon that are like 100 characters long or random letters. For example, my link for Blue Host hosting is fairly long but it's a redirect using Pretty Link and it's just smartpassiveincome.com/bluehost and that's it and it will redirect through that affiliate link. It's really easy to memorize, easy to say, people don't have to rewind my podcast or write it all down, it's really easy. It also keeps track of all the clicks. I'll often have one blog post that is promoting or recommending one product but I'll have four different links for it. So I have the first link, the image link, the link below, and then the link at the very bottom so I can kind of see which one gets clicked on the most, and then I can optimize it and test and things like that.

Another one that I like is a premium plug-in called *Backup Buddy*. I've lost a lot of stuff before because of things crashing for reasons I have no control over and Backup Buddy is great. It's a paid plugin. There are other free ones out there but I like this one because the support is great. It also allows me to, not only save into my database, but to save it off my website in to Amazon S3 or Dropbox or both. My business is what pays the bills, it's what's paying for my kids college. I have to really protect it. You know you always say "*Oh it's not going to happen to me*" but it could. So that's why I take really good care to make sure things are backed up just in case.

Another good one is *WordPress SEO* by Joost Devalk from **yoast.com.** I know a lot of people promote the All-in-One SEO plug-in and that is a great one too, but that's the one that I use now and it's really robust and it does a lot of things from the sitemaps to the permalinks. So I would recommend checking that out and seeing if it's worth it for you. There's also videos on **yoost.com** about how to actually configure those.

Conclusion

I want to congratulate you on making it all the way through this comprehensive guide on everything WordPress. It can seem overwhelming when you're first trying to figure it out. However, I promise that it becomes really simple after only a few uses.

Give it a shot, don't be afraid to play around with it a little, and just get started. You will be amazed at what you can accomplish with this powerful platform.

At this point, you should have a pretty good overview of how to get your first site online. There's no reason that you shouldn't have it up an running by the end of the day today. So I highly recommend that you take the time now to actually follow the steps outlined in the book and get your website online while it's still hot in your mind. This is the best time to start.

If you're interested in watching "over-the-shoulder" videos of exactly how to set this stuff up yourself, please check out the seven day WordPress training course that I put together for you at http://www.thewpclassroom.com/wprevealed/. It's completely free to get started and it's exclusive to buyers of this book.

Thanks so much for allowing me to walk you through WordPress. I hope you've learned a lot and I can't wait to hear your feedback. Any feedback sent to me via email, Twitter, or Facebook, will be taken to heart and I'll do my best to add any questions in to the next version of this book.

Resources

Free WordPress Training Videos:

http://www.TheWPClassroom.com/wprevealed/

My Personal Blog:

http://www.BusinessAndBlogs.com/

The WordPress Classroom on Facebook

http://www.Facebook.com/WordPressClassroom

My Personal Facebook:

http://www.Facebook.com/BusinessAndBlogs

Follow Me On Twitter:

http://www.Twitter.com/MattRWolfe

Please Leave A Review On Amazon.com

If you enjoyed this book. Please do me a huge favor and leave a review over on Amazon.com. All of your feedback is greatly appreciated.

Feel free to tell your friends about this book as well. :) I can use all the help and promotion I can get.

Acknowledgments

There are so many people that I'd like to thank that helped make this resource possible.

For starters, I must thank my wife, Alana, who put up with me typing away at the computer until 3:00 am in the same room she was trying to sleep in. Creating a better life for the both of us has always been my motivation for working ungodly hours to reach deadlines and to expand my business. I love you Alana and I couldn't have been able to do any of what I've done so far without your support and encouragement.

Thank you to my parents, Rick and Trisha Wolfe, for always encouraging me to pursue my own business. You taught me about running a business and managing employees. Working at the shutter company with you guys really prepared me to handle any situation that could arise in my own business. I'm so grateful to have been raised in a household of entrepreneurs and to have really seen the ups and downs of business before having to go at it by myself. Thanks for buying our first computer when I was at a really early age. Instead of pulling me away from the computer, you helped me to nurture the talent I was building and encouraged me to learn more and more about it. You guys are the reason I have the skills that I have today.

Thanks so much to Carol and Alan Beilstein for giving us a place to live while in our "transition phase" from one house to another. You've been so kind and hospitable and I really couldn't thank you enough! This is what I was doing on many of those days when I was closed up in the back bedroom, typing away. You've been so supportive and I love the fact that you've always taken such an interest in my business and you're always looking for ways to help out and support it. I can't thank you guys enough!

I'd also like to thank Sean Vossler, Ori Bengal, Pat Flynn, Glen Allsopp, Casey Zeman, and Kim Roach for so graciously allowing me to interview them on how they use WordPress. I've learned just as much out of this experience myself as I hope I've managed to teach others. You guys rock! Thanks again for the contribution!

To Jeff Stewart, Steve Dougherty, and Jay Mueller... You guys have helped me keep The WordPress Classroom alive while I took time away to write this book and learn more about being an author and a publisher. Without you guys, I would have never been able to make this happen. Thank you so much!

To Josh Bartlett, my genius business partner, who helped name the book and has provided me with an unending amount of support and feedback on my business. Josh is the one person I turn to when I'm feeling unsure about my business or I need a new idea to spark sales. Josh always has the answer and he's always there to make sure I keep my business moving in the right direction.

And to all my friends in the online business world that have offered me advice and encouragement along the way... Joe Fier, Josh Grillo, Joey Kissimmee, Henry Evans, Thomas Mangum, Justin Brooke, Chris Farrell, Stephen Renton, Jon Barrett, Clive Cable, Michael Dunlop, James Dyson, David Sinick, Mario Brown, Jason Moffatt, Michael Taggart, David Walker, Bradley Will, Russell Yermal, Devon Brown, AJ Silvers, Christine McDannel, Ali Kahn, Omar Martin, Melinda Martin, Alex Jeffreys, Seth Larrabee, and anyone else who's given me advice and support along the way. This community that we've all created has formed some amazing friendships and has really turned in to a platform where we can all lift each other up.

And finally, to all of the thought leaders and entrepreneurs whom I don't know personally but have inspired me immensely... Tim Ferriss, Robert Kiyosaki, Richard Branson, Tony Robbins, Andre Chaperon, Joe Polish, Ryan Deiss, Perry Belcher, Rich Schefren, Robert Cialdini, Michael Gerber, Gary Vaynerchuk, and, of course, Matt Mullenweg, the original creator of WordPress.

Thank you all so much!

19076802R00072

Made in the USA
Lexington, KY
05 December 2012